# Head to Toe

# Head to Toe

My Body and
How It Works

How?

What?

Thames & Hudson

# Questions from head to toe ...

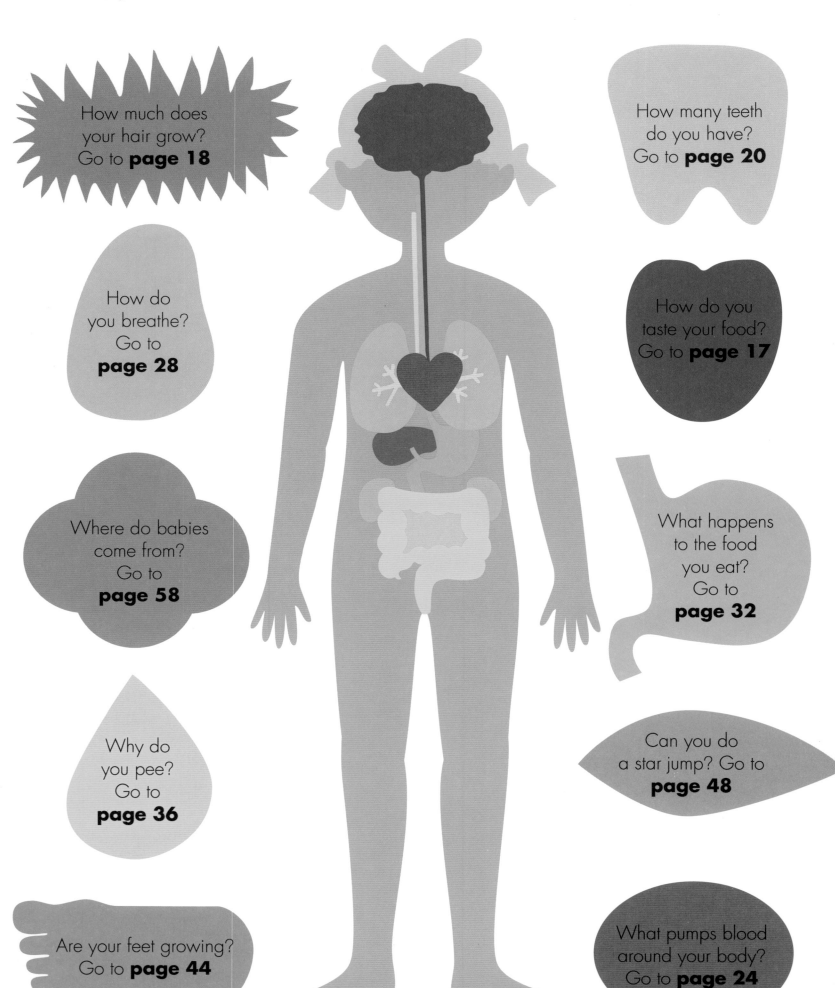

How much does your hair grow? Go to **page 18**

How many teeth do you have? Go to **page 20**

How do you breathe? Go to **page 28**

How do you taste your food? Go to **page 17**

Where do babies come from? Go to **page 58**

What happens to the food you eat? Go to **page 32**

Why do you pee? Go to **page 36**

Can you do a star jump? Go to **page 48**

Are your feet growing? Go to **page 44**

What pumps blood around your body? Go to **page 24**

# Where to find out!

# How to use this book

Are you ready to go on a journey through your body from head to toe, inside and out?

10 inches

## Say hello to Koko

Hi, I'm Koko. I'm your guide. I love finding out new things. Do you?

8 inches

6 inches

How tall are you? Measure this book against yourself. How many books high are you?

4 inches

Hi, I'm Koko's friend Alex. I'm listening to my heartbeat. Put your hand to your chest to feel yours.

2 inches

# When you see ...

… ask a grown-up
to help you.

… get ready to
do things.

**Where next?**
**Your brain** controls your muscles.
Go to **My muscles, page 46**

… go to another page
to find out more.

# Meet the explorers

The three explorers travel inside your body and
show you how it works. They love adventures!

Look! It's this way.
Everyone ready?
Follow me!

Well, let me just
check the map and
find the way.

Come on guys, let's
go! We've got lots
of exploring to do.

# OK! Let's go ...

# My brain

## Count from one to ten. Now move your legs and dance!

What makes you do these things? It's your brain – the part of your body that is in charge! This picture shows inside your brain.

Tap your head. That's your skull keeping your brain safe.

move

Hey! I've found the part of the brain you use to think.

think

I remember where I put my favorite toy. Where's yours?

remember

Different parts of your brain control different things, such as thinking. What else does your brain control?

Look! Messages are going up and down to the rest of the body.

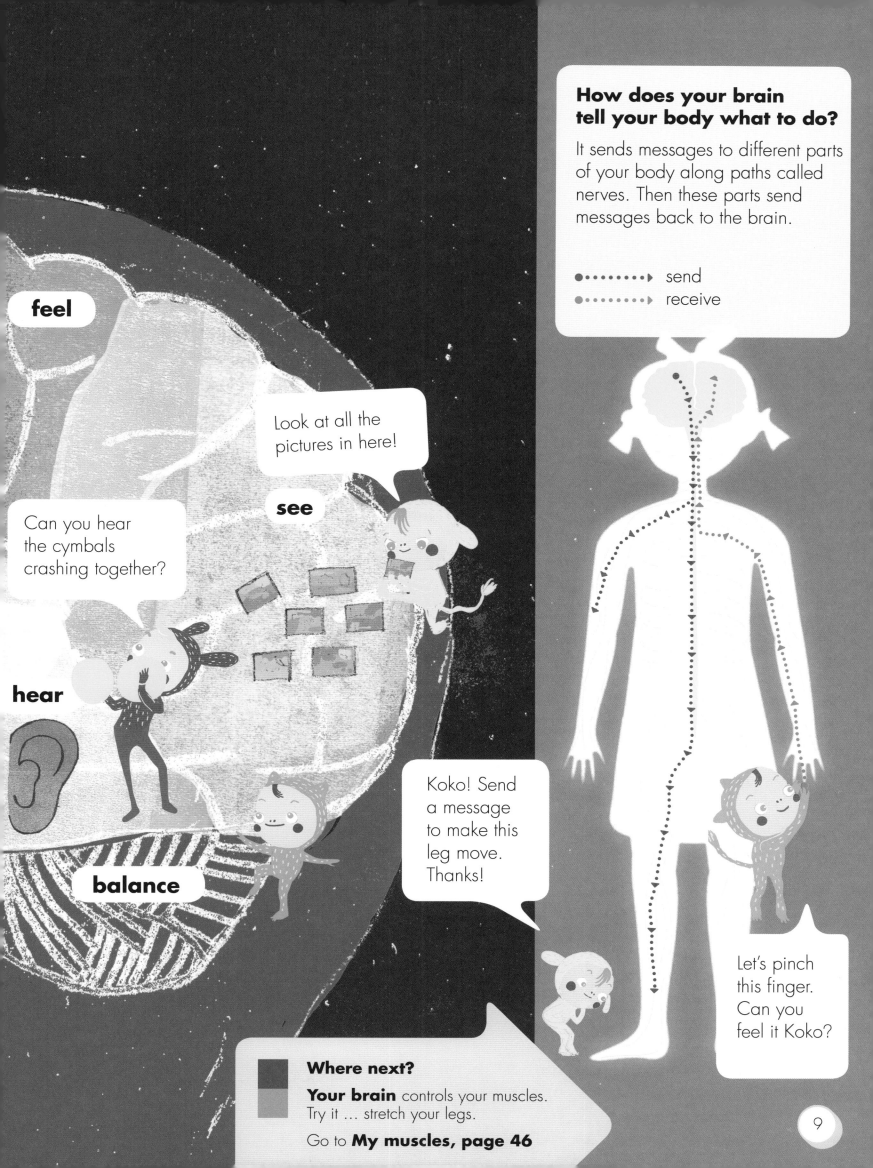

**feel**

Look at all the pictures in here!

Can you hear the cymbals crashing together?

**see**

**hear**

**balance**

Koko! Send a message to make this leg move. Thanks!

**How does your brain tell your body what to do?**

It sends messages to different parts of your body along paths called nerves. Then these parts send messages back to the brain.

●········▶ send
●········▶ receive

Let's pinch this finger. Can you feel it Koko?

**Where next?**

**Your brain** controls your muscles. Try it ... stretch your legs.

Go to **My muscles, page 46**

# Remote-control brain game

Play this game and find out how your brain controls your body.

**You will need**

*cardboard, crayons, dress-up clothes, a friend*

**1** Make a cardboard remote control. Write on simple orders. Dress up or stay in your everyday clothes.

**2** Decide who is the brain and who is the body. Shout out orders – turn, jump up, grab a chair!

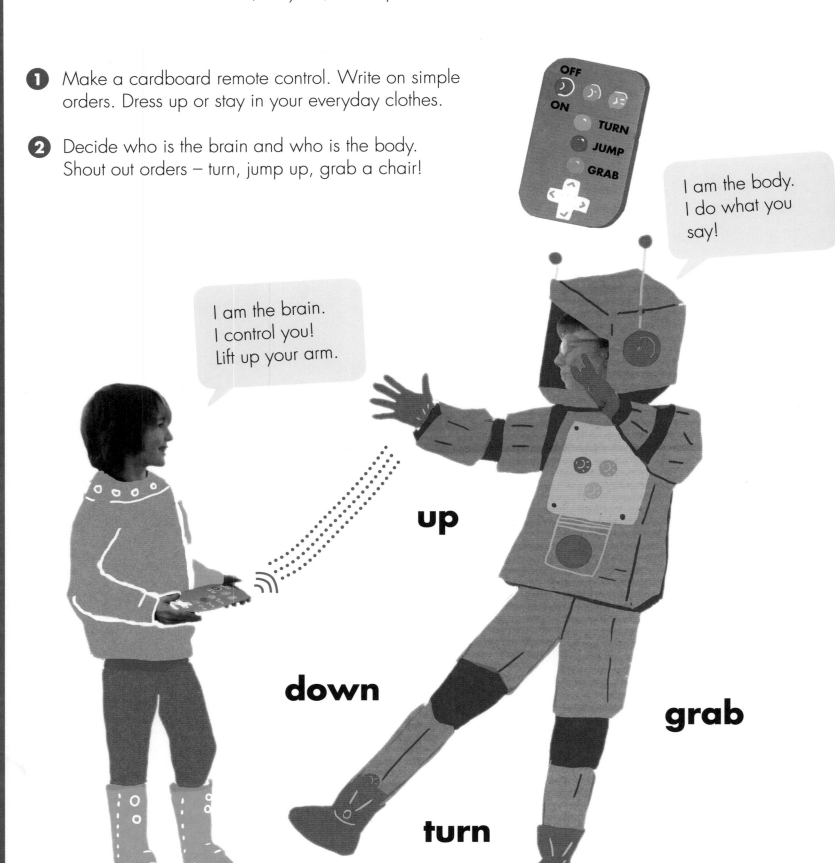

I am the brain.
I control you!
Lift up your arm.

I am the body.
I do what you say!

up

down

grab

turn

# Memory game

Use your brainpower! How good is your memory?

Look at the objects on the tray for one minute.
Try to remember them all.

Now turn the page …

What is missing from the tray? Did you get it right?

## Make your own game

Play with friends

### You will need
*paper plate*
*ten small objects*

**1** Ask a friend to look at the plate for one minute.

**2** Without your friend seeing, take away one object. Can your friend remember which one is missing?

Can you tell which object is missing from the plate on the right?

# My senses

## How can you tell what's safe and what's dangerous?

You use your senses. They tell you all about your world. You have five senses. They are taste, touch, smell, sight and hearing.

Alex can see the bird and hear it singing.

**Match it**

Can you tell which senses Alex is using?
Match the words to the pictures.
Which sense is he not using?

**TOUCH** skin   **SEE** eye   **SMELL** nose   **TASTE** tongue   **HEAR** ear

# My senses

Koko and her friend Alex are having a picnic.

What animals can they **see** at the pond?
What prickly things should they not **touch**?
What sweet things can they **taste** for lunch?
What can they **hear** singing?
Something **smells** really bad! What is it?

Make up your own questions about the picture. What else is there to see, hear, smell, taste and touch?

# Touch and guess

What's hiding in the box?

## You will need
*cardboard box, scissors, different objects*

**Adult help needed!**

Ask a grown-up to cut a hole in the box and to place different objects inside.

Describe what you feel. Is it rough? Is it smooth? Is it soft, tickly or hard? What is it? Does it bite?!

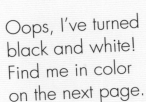

Oops, I've turned black and white! Find me in color on the next page.

# Eye trick

Your eyes can play tricks on you.

Look at the blue pattern for a few seconds. Can you see some gray dots?

# Taste test

What senses do you use when you eat your food?

Adult help needed!

## You will need

*apple, pear, peeled onion, celery, knife, blindfold*

**1** Ask a grown-up to chop the food into small pieces.

**2** Tie on the blindfold.

**3** Pinch your nose. Taste one piece, then another.

This is like when I have a cold. I can't taste anything!

Can you taste the difference? No! Your sense of taste works with your senses of smell and sight to help you enjoy your food.

# My hair

## What do you think hair is for?

To make us look good?
To help us recognize each other?
To keep us warm? To protect us?
Well, it's all of these things!

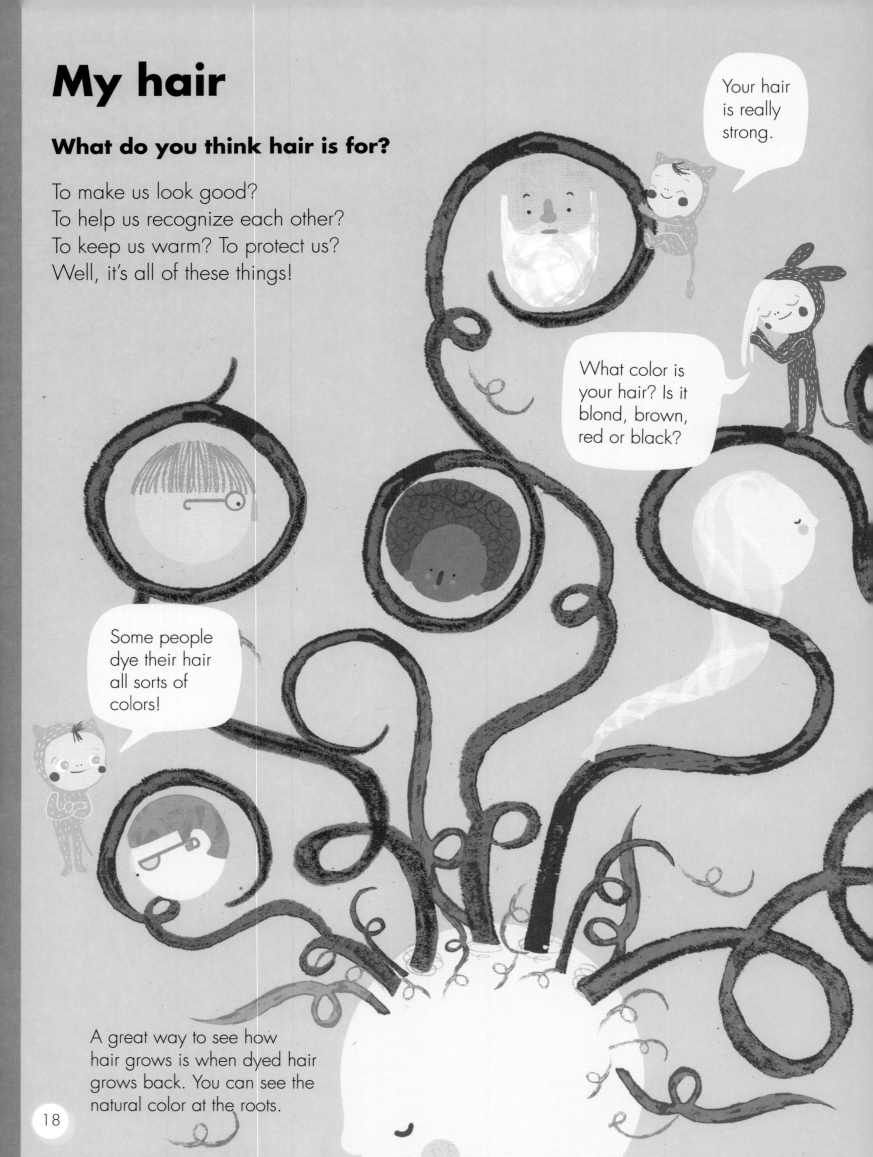

Your hair is really strong.

What color is your hair? Is it blond, brown, red or black?

Some people dye their hair all sorts of colors!

A great way to see how hair grows is when dyed hair grows back. You can see the natural color at the roots.

An adult's hair grows about 6 inches a year. Look at how long this is on the ruler.

What shape is your hair? Is it straight, wavy or curly?

Older people can lose their hair, or go bald. Can you find a bald person here?

**Where next?**

**Your skin** can be different colors, like your hair or eyes.

Go to **My skin, page 40**

## Growing up

When you grow up, you grow more hair, especially boys. One day, a boy could grow a mustache or a beard.

### Finger mustache

10 inches

8 inches

**1** Draw a mustache on your finger with a washable felt-tip pen.

**2** Try out different designs on each finger.

6 inches

### Mustache postcard

4 inches

2 inches

**1** Draw a face on a piece of paper.

**2** Cut out a mustache from furry fabric.

**3** Stick the mustache on the face to make your very own mustache character!

19

# My teeth

## How do you eat a crunchy snack?

You use your teeth to cut, tear and chew your food into smaller pieces. By the age of six most children have 20 baby teeth. These fall out and 32 adult teeth grow.

How many teeth can you count in in this big mouth?

I am falling out!

Front teeth are for cutting. They have sharp edges.

Look! Here's a space for a new tooth.

Oh no! Horrible germs are eating a picnic of leftover food. Germs harm teeth. Better call the toothbrush.

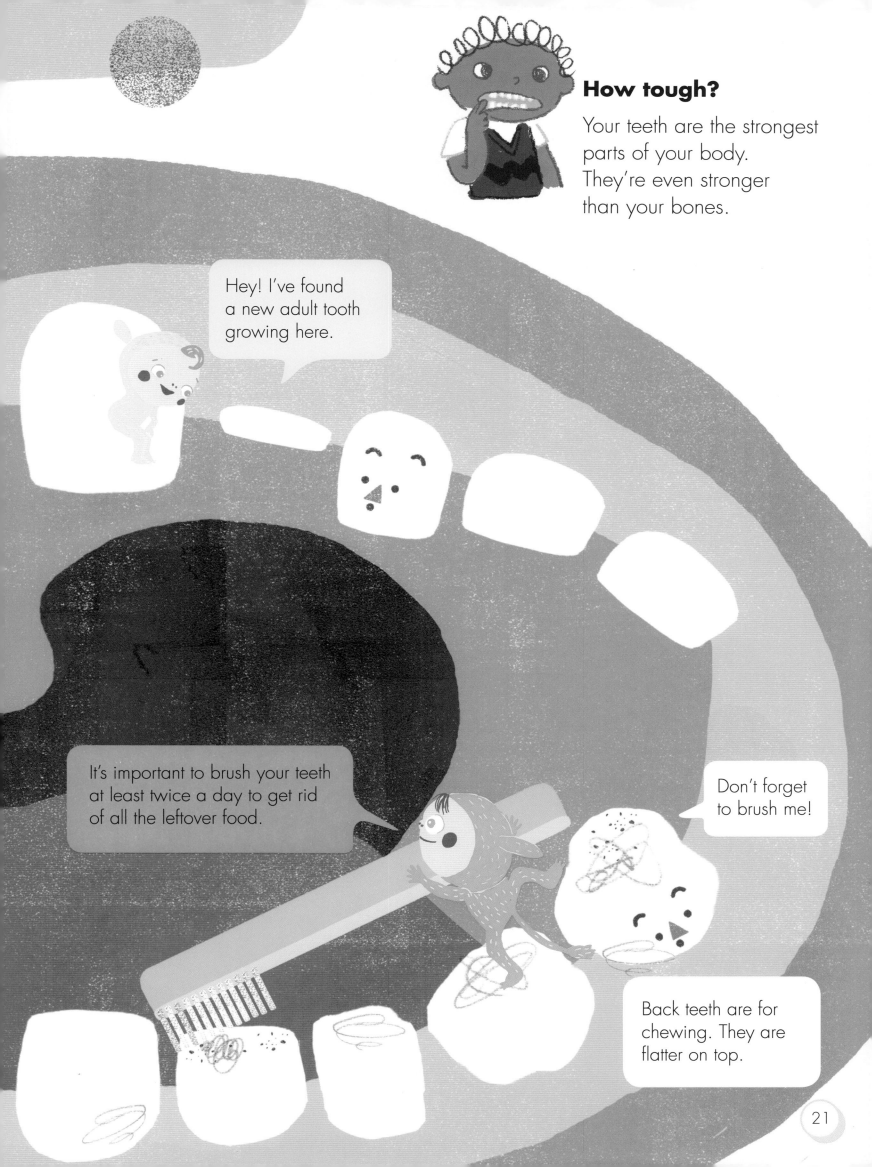

**How tough?**

Your teeth are the strongest parts of your body. They're even stronger than your bones.

# My voice

## Sing your favorite song loudly!

The singing sounds come from inside your throat.
They are made by your vocal cords.

While you are singing, place your hand on your throat. Can you feel your throat wobbling?

Look! There's a tube inside with stretchy parts. These are your vocal cords.

When you sing, your vocal cords close just like in this picture.

When you stop singing, your vocal cords open.

**vocal cords closed**　　　　**vocal cords open**

# Make voice boxes

## High or low?

As you grow, your voice changes. Boys often have lower voices than girls.

## You will need
*two plastic cups of different widths, four rubber bands*

**1** Strap two rubber bands across each cup. Put them close together.

**2** Pluck them with your fingers to make sounds.

Are the sounds from the two cups different? Which cup makes the lower sound?

# Make a paper whistle

## You will need
*piece of paper 4 inches long and 2 inches wide, scissors*

**Adult help needed!**

**1**

Fold the rectangle of paper in half.

**2**

Cut out a small triangle on the folded side.

**3**

Fold back the two edges and place them against your mouth.

Blow hard!

**Where next?**

**Your body** makes lots of sounds.
Go to **Body noises, page 62**

# My heart and blood

## What beats in your body day and night?

Your heart pumps blood around your body. The blood travels around like a car on a wiggly road.

**Where are we?**

**Let's follow the beating sound.**

**Trace the journey of the blood with your finger. Follow the arrows.**

### What's in blood?

red blood cells

white blood cells

platelets

Find them in the picture to learn what they do.

### Blood has many jobs

 It warms up your body.

 It carries food to every part.

 It picks up waste and takes it away.

Look at the picture to find out what else blood does.

**I eat germs.**

**When your heart beats, it makes a pulse. Press your finger to your wrist to feel your pulse.**

# Cookie people

## You will need

all-purpose flour........ 1½ cups
baking soda......... 1 teaspoon
butter (cut up) ....6½ tablespoons
brown sugar.............. ½ cup
egg ................................ 1
golden syrup .... 4 tablespoons
allspice .............. 1 teaspoon
cinnamon............ 1 teaspoon
red and white frosting,
dried fruit

**Adult help needed!**

## What to do

**1** Preheat the oven to 350°. Put all the ingredients except the dried fruit and frosting into a mixing bowl.

**2** Mix into a thick dough with your hands. Roll out the dough to the thickness of your finger.

**3** Using a cookie cutter, cut out four people.

**4** Place them on an ungreased baking tray and bake for 10 minutes until golden.

**5** Leave to cool. Pipe on red and white frosting to show blood traveling through your body.

**6** Press on a dried-fruit heart and eat!

# Body map

Imagine criss-crossing roads inside your body, delivering blood to every part.

① Take an old road map and cut out a body shape.

② Draw on a heart. Can you see how your blood travels now?

# Koko's scab story

Koko fell over and cut her knee. She started to bleed, but then her body healed itself!

Oooh! My knee is bleeding. It hurts.

Look! The blood's dried up. I've got a scab.

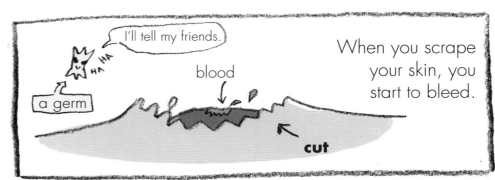

I'll tell my friends.

a germ

blood

cut

When you scrape your skin, you start to bleed.

a gang of germs

Then the blood dries and makes a scab.

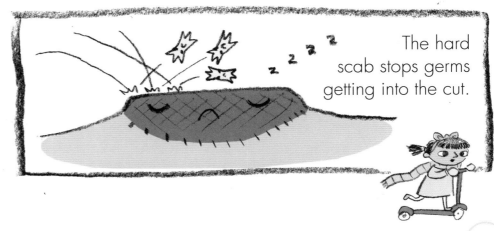

The hard scab stops germs getting into the cut.

# Breathing

**Ready? Take a deep breath in. Don't forget to breathe out!**

Follow the explorers to find out what happens inside your body when you breathe in and out. Start at number 1.

How long can you hold your breath for? Not that long! That's because we must breathe air to stay alive.

Your lungs are like an accordion, sucking in air when you breathe in and pushing it back when you breathe out.

**5** You have two lungs, so which way does the air go? It goes both ways!

You breathe in and out all the time, even when you're asleep. Most of the time, you don't even think about it.

**6** The insides of your lungs are similar to sponges and take good things from the air.

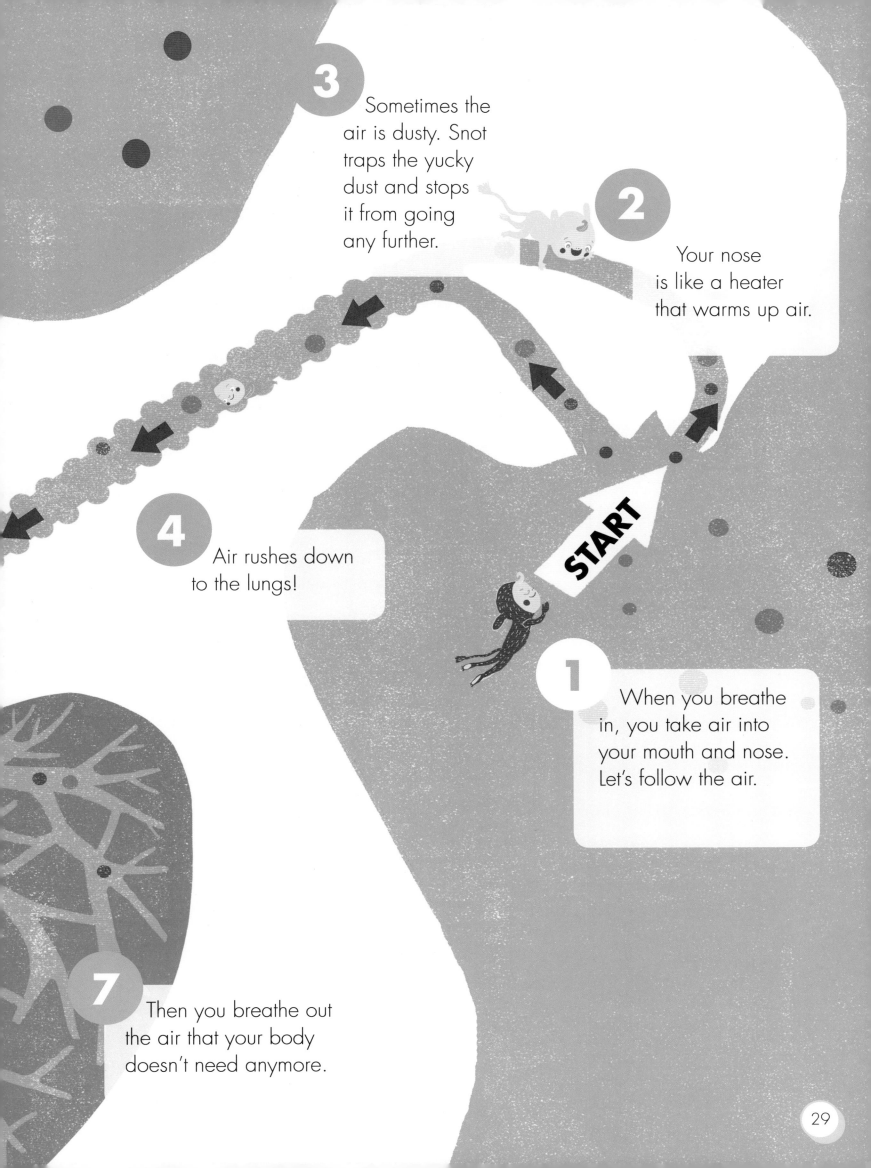

**3** Sometimes the air is dusty. Snot traps the yucky dust and stops it from going any further.

**2** Your nose is like a heater that warms up air.

START

**4** Air rushes down to the lungs!

**1** When you breathe in, you take air into your mouth and nose. Let's follow the air.

**7** Then you breathe out the air that your body doesn't need anymore.

# Air from the lungs

There are lots of things we can do with the air that we have in our lungs.

Blow up a balloon. All the air inside has come from your lungs!

When you play a trumpet or horn, you blow air out from your lungs.

# Bubble experiment

Air is invisible, but you can see it with this clever trick.

**You will need**

straw

glass of water

1 Blow through the straw into the glass of water.

2 What can you see? Lots of bubbles filled with air.

Count how long you can blow air bubbles for.

# Koko's huff-and-puff experiment

Koko marches up and down the stairs over and over again.
Do you think she starts breathing faster or slower?

When you exercise, you need more air, so your brain
orders you to breathe faster. This gives you the extra air.

Now you try it. But watch out – don't run!

# Eating

## After you've eaten your dinner, where does all the food go?

Well, it goes on a big adventure through your body! Koko has eaten some vegetables. Take a look inside her body and find out what happens.

Tasty food gives me lots of energy to run around and play!

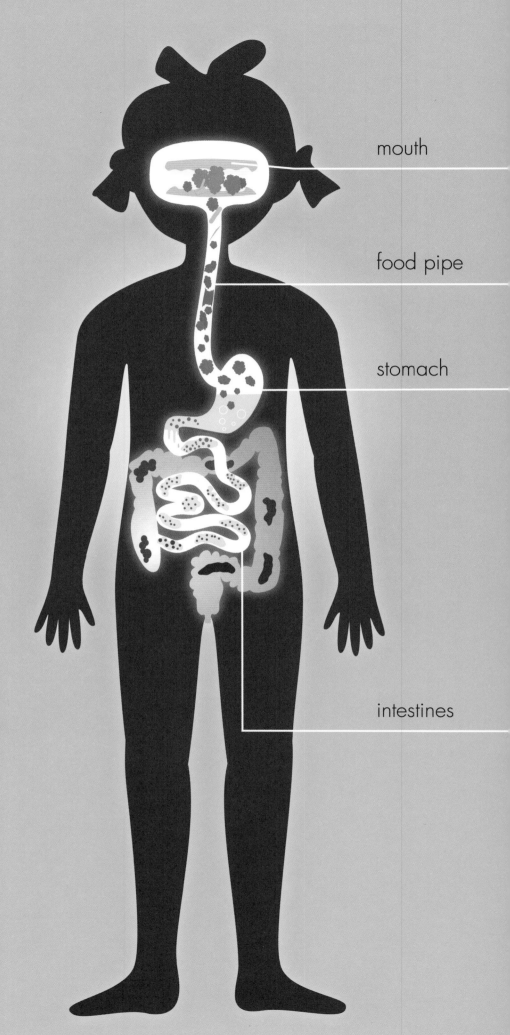

mouth

food pipe

stomach

intestines

Koko cuts and chews the vegetables into small pieces with her teeth. She tastes if the food is salty or sweet with her tongue.

Koko swallows and the pieces go down a long tube.

In her stomach, the vegetables mix with juices and break down into even tinier pieces.

These tiny pieces go into a long, wiggly tube called the intestines. Then even tinier bits of food travel in blood around the body.

The leftover bits continue through the tube and come out as poop.

**Where next?**

Your blood carries the food's good bits around your body.

Go to **My heart and blood, page 24**

## Spot the foods

Look at what these foods do for you. Find them in the picture.

These foods give you the energy to run and play.

Fruit and vegetables are full of vitamins to keep you healthy.

These foods help your body to grow and heal.

Which three things would you pick for a healthy snack?

# Going to the bathroom

## Play the busy body game!

Food is delivered to different parts of your body. Your body takes the good bits from the food and gets rid of the waste. This waste comes out when you go to the bathroom.

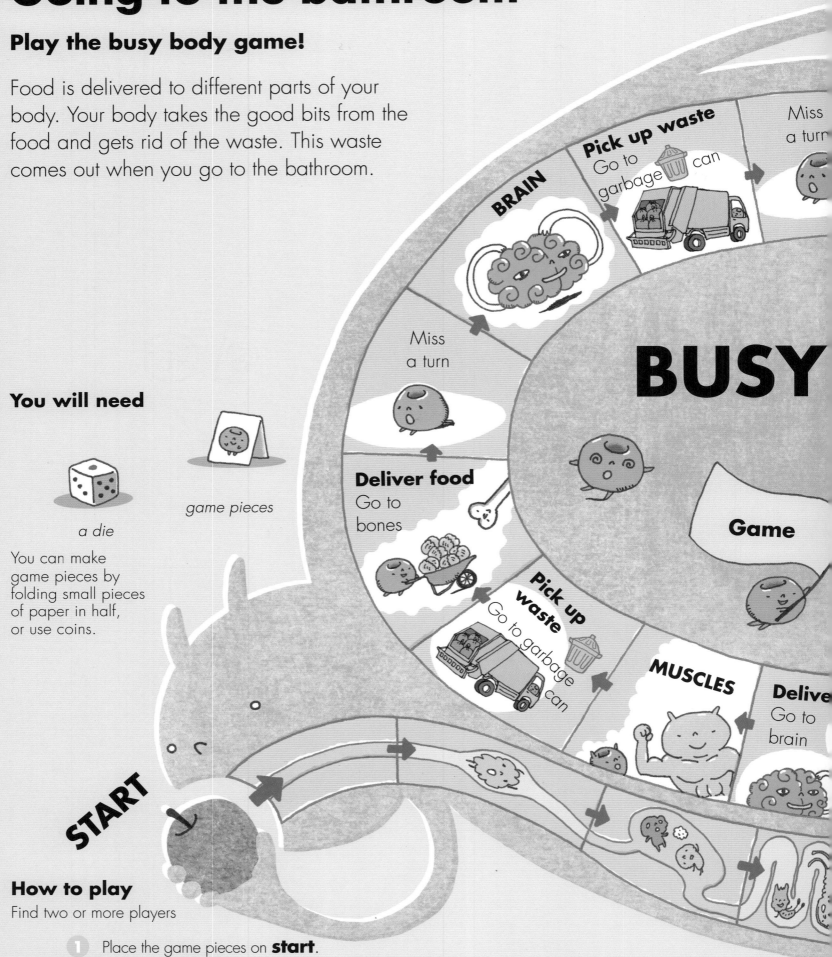

**You will need**

*a die*

*game pieces*

You can make game pieces by folding small pieces of paper in half, or use coins.

**Pick up waste** Go to garbage can

BRAIN

Miss a turn

Miss a turn

BUSY

Deliver food Go to bones

Game

**Pick up waste** Go to garbage can

MUSCLES

Deliver Go to brain

START

## How to play

Find two or more players

1. Place the game pieces on **start**.

2. Take turns to throw the die. Follow the blue arrows and the instructions. Keep going round until you land on the garbage can.

3. The first one to pee or poop wins!

BONES

Deliver food
Go to muscles

GARBAGE CAN

BODY

Go around delivering food and picking up waste.

On your next turn:

if you throw a 2, poop.

if you throw a 1, pee.

If you throw any other number, go round again.

Pick up food

Pick up waste
Go to garbage can

WIN!
POOP

Hurry up!

Go for a poop

Go for a pee

Nearly there!

WIN!
PEE

**Where next?**

Blood carries food around your body.

Go to **My heart and blood, page 24**

# Pee and poop

## Did you know that your pee can change color?

If your pee contains lots of water it is pale yellow.
If it contains lots of waste it is darker yellow.
Most people don't drink water overnight so
their pee is darker first thing in the morning.

## We poop throughout our lives ...

Babies poop into
their diapers.

What do you do
while you poop?

Grown-ups poop.
Sometimes they read
while they poop.

**Can you match the poop to the owner?**

A clue: Koko likes to eat corn.

**Uggh! I've just farted!**

**Why does it smell so bad?**

Even Grandpa is pooping.

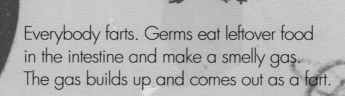

Everybody farts. Germs eat leftover food in the intestine and make a smelly gas. The gas builds up and comes out as a fart.

# My skin

**Your skin covers your whole body and holds it together.**

Koko is thinking about her skin and all the ways it looks after her.

My skin is **waterproof**. If it weren't, I'd fill up with water when I have a bath.

My skin is like a suit of armor. It **protects** me from germs.

My skin is **stretchy**. If it weren't, I would be stiff like a scarecrow.

My skin **cools** me down and stops my body from getting too hot in the sun.

My skin lets me **feel**. I can feel the hot sand between my toes.

# Fingerprint stamps

Make fingerprint people!

## You will need
*poster paint or ink pad, paper*

**1** Dip your finger in the paint or press it on the ink pad. Then press your finger on the paper.

**2** When the prints are dry, draw on arms, legs and faces.

## Spot the difference

Everybody has a different fingerprint pattern. Make your print, then ask a friend to do the same. Can you spot the differences?

People have different colored skin. What color is yours?

**Where next?**

Your skin protects you from germs.

Go to **Koko's scab story, page 27**

# My bones

## Knock knock! The hard parts of your body are your bones.

Together, all your bones make a big frame called a skeleton. Without it, you would be floppy and fall down.

Turn the book around to see a picture of your skeleton.

Here's the skull. It's like a hard helmet protecting your soft brain.

Your ribs protect your heart and lungs.

I found a shoulder bone.

Can you feel the bones in your arm? Point to them on the skeleton.

## Find the bones

Where are these bones in the skeleton?

Your hip lets your leg move.

This is the knee joint. A joint is where bones make contact. Can you find other joints?

I'm sitting on the biggest bone in your body.

Look, the bones in your arm work like the arm of a digger.

### Where next?

You use your muscles to make your bones move.

Go to **My muscles, page 46**

43

# How do I grow?

As you get older, you grow taller.
This is because your bones grow.

**1**

**2**

This is Shen …

… and these are her favorite shoes.

**3**

Wherever Shen went, her shoes went too!

**4**

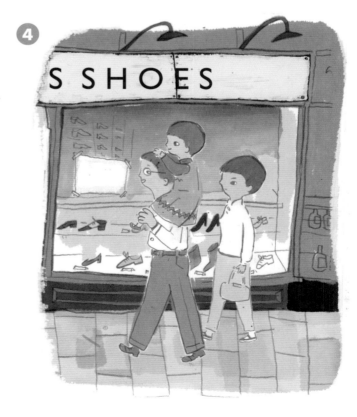

Sometimes, Shen and her mom picked up Shen's dad from work. They always walked past Shen's favorite shoe store.

**5**

One day, Shen could no longer fit into her favorite shoes! They were too tight. What was happening?

**6**

That night, Shen dreamed her shoes were shrinking. They shrank so much that her teddy bear could wear them!

**7**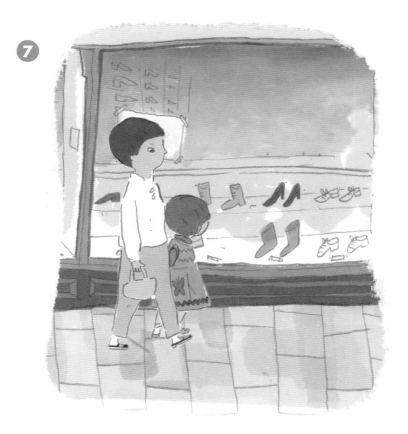

Shen's mom took Shen to her favorite shoe store. "The shoes aren't shrinking," she laughed, "Your feet are growing! Let's buy a new pair."

**8**

Shen loved her new bigger shoes. These were her favorite shoes now. Wherever Shen went, the shoes went too!

# My muscles

**Can you touch your head and then your toes? Try it now.**

Your muscles help to make you move!

Look at all the things we are doing with our muscles!

I'm using my leg muscles to cycle.

We are using our arm muscles to throw and catch the balls.

We are using lots of muscles when we pretend to be acrobats.

But how do muscles work?

Muscles pull your bones. They work a bit like the strings on a puppet.

Look at the muscles in my arm. Can you feel your muscles?

## Muscle power

This is what happens inside your body when you bend your arm and then straighten it.

**bend your arm**

**straighten your arm**

Your muscle gets shorter ...

Your muscle relaxes ...

... and the bone gets pulled up.

... and the bone goes down.

# Get moving

**Play muscle gym**

Practice each action, then ask a friend to shout out the actions in different orders. If you go wrong, it's your friend's turn!

**1** Ready?

**2** Do a star jump.

**4** Run on the spot.

**5** Kick the ball.

**6** Swing the racket.

I know. It's your bottom and it's called gluteus maximus!

I wonder what is the biggest muscle in your body?

**Where next?**

Most of your muscles are attached to your bones.

Go to **My bones, page 42**

## How many muscles?

You have about 60 muscles in your face. These muscles help you to make faces. Make these faces to show if you are happy, sad, surprised or angry.

**3** Go for a swim.

**7** Skate round and round.

Your heart is a muscle too!

What other funny faces can you make?

# Body hopscotch game

Let's play a game to make your muscles work!

**Adult help needed!**

## You will need
*a stone*
*piece of chalk*
*open space*
*someone to play with*

## Get started
Check with an adult first, then draw a body shape on the ground. Split it into squares and number each one.

## How to play

**1** Throw the stone onto square 1 and hop over it to square 2.

**2** Hop from numbered square to numbered square up to the head.

**3** Turn around and hop back in the same way.

## It's your friend's turn if ...

– your stone doesn't land in the right square.
– you hop on the square where your stone is.
– you touch the white lines with your feet.

## The winner is ...

the first person to throw the stone onto all eight squares.

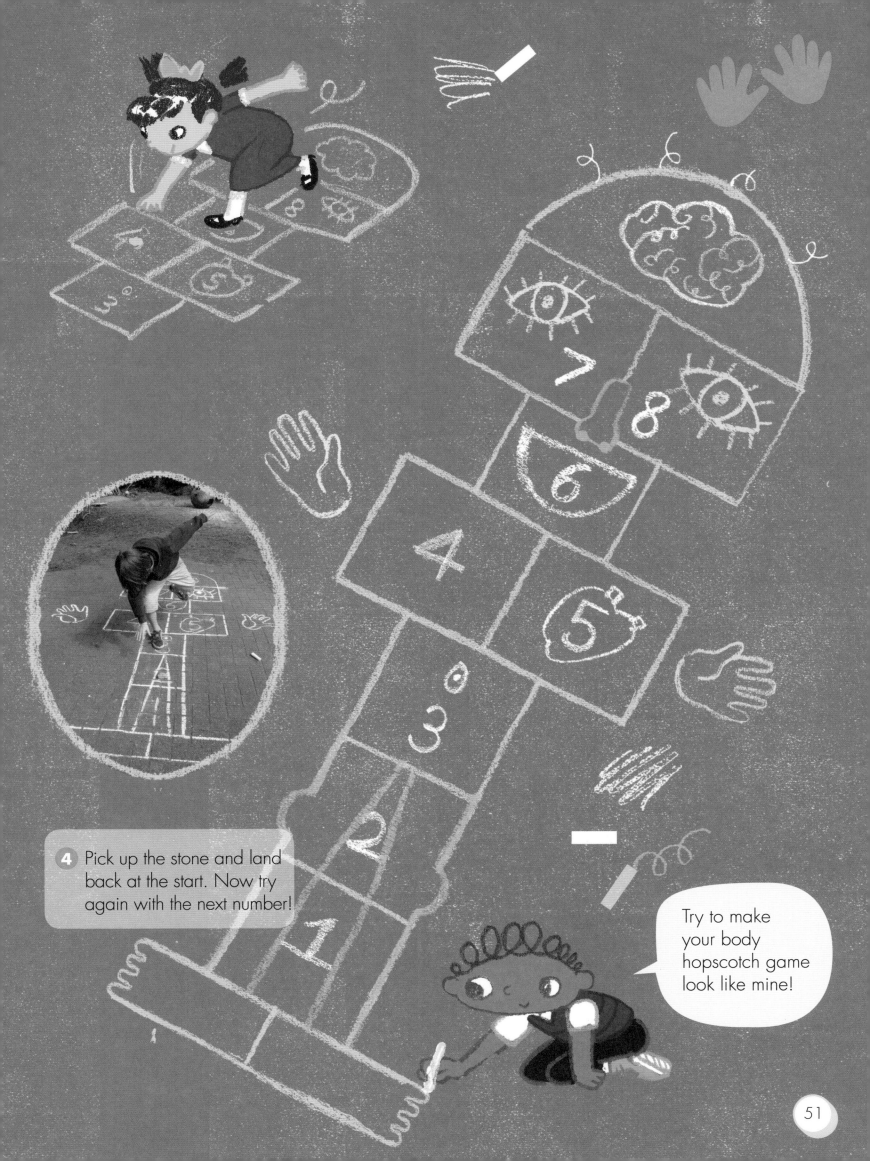

# Staying healthy

Early to rise
for a healthy start,
a healthy body and
a healthy heart.

Healthy food
and lots to drink,
gives your brain
the chance to think.

Take a shower,
have a bath,
splash and swim,
and have a laugh.

Cycle, walk,
skip and run –
healthy sports are
so much fun.

Early to bed
will help you stay,
fit and healthy
every day.

Be kind to others
and watch yourself grow,
happy and healthy from
head down to toe!

# Being sick

## Everybody feels unwell sometimes.

When you're sick, you go to a doctor in a hospital. What's happening in this hospital? Who's having an eye test? How many bandaged animals can you count? Who has just had babies?

## Eye spy

Play eye spy with your friends. To start you off, find …

a fox with its leg in a cast

a duck on the phone

a sick turkey

EMERGENCY

54

# Sleeping

What time do you go to sleep? Do you take a favorite toy to bed with you?

**Sleep helps to keep your body healthy and to make you grow.**

Try to sleep for 10 or 12 hours each night. You'll feel bright and fresh the next morning.

I'm trying to make the bones grow longer!

Your bones keep growing during the night.

Koko is asleep. What things can you see happening? Do you snore in your sleep like Koko?

Let's finish mashing up this apple and store the energy for tomorrow.

While you are asleep, parts of your body keep working hard.

**Where next?**

Your body makes noises when you are asleep and when you are awake.

Go to **Body noises, page 62**

# Babies

Where does a baby come from?

A baby comes from its mother's stomach.

**It's hard to imagine, but you were once a tiny baby.**

Before you were born, you were so small that you could live inside your mom.

To make a baby, you need an egg from the mother and a sperm from the father. The egg and sperm join together to make the baby.

sperm    egg

This is what a dad's sperm looks like.

This is what a mom's egg looks like.

START

When people are grown up, they can have babies!

Look! The tiny baby is starting to grow.

Now the baby is nearly ready to come out of the mother's tummy.

# ROUND AND ROUND

**Follow the circle around to see the tiny baby grow, be born and become a grown-up.**

birth

The baby is born and grows into a toddler.

The toddler grows into a child and then a teenager.

# My feelings

How do you feel today? Sing along with this rhyme.

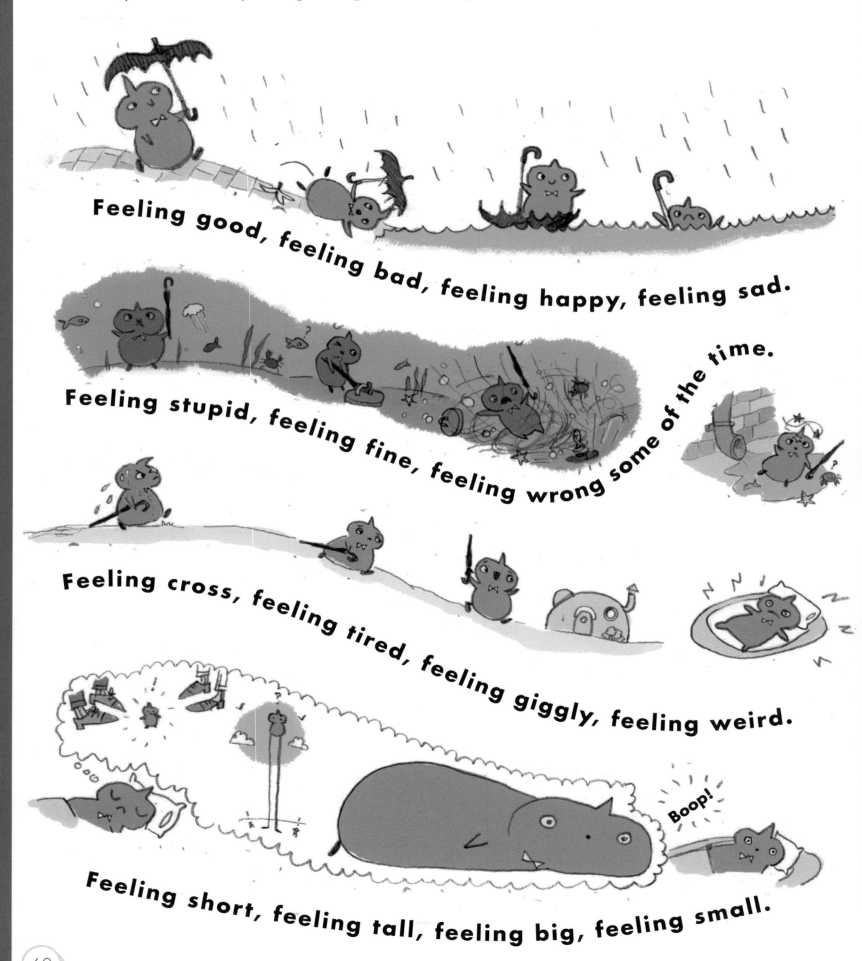

Feeling good, feeling bad, feeling happy, feeling sad.

Feeling stupid, feeling fine, feeling wrong some of the time.

Feeling cross, feeling tired, feeling giggly, feeling weird.

Boop!

Feeling short, feeling tall, feeling big, feeling small.

Feeling well, feeling sick, feeling lazy, feeling quick.

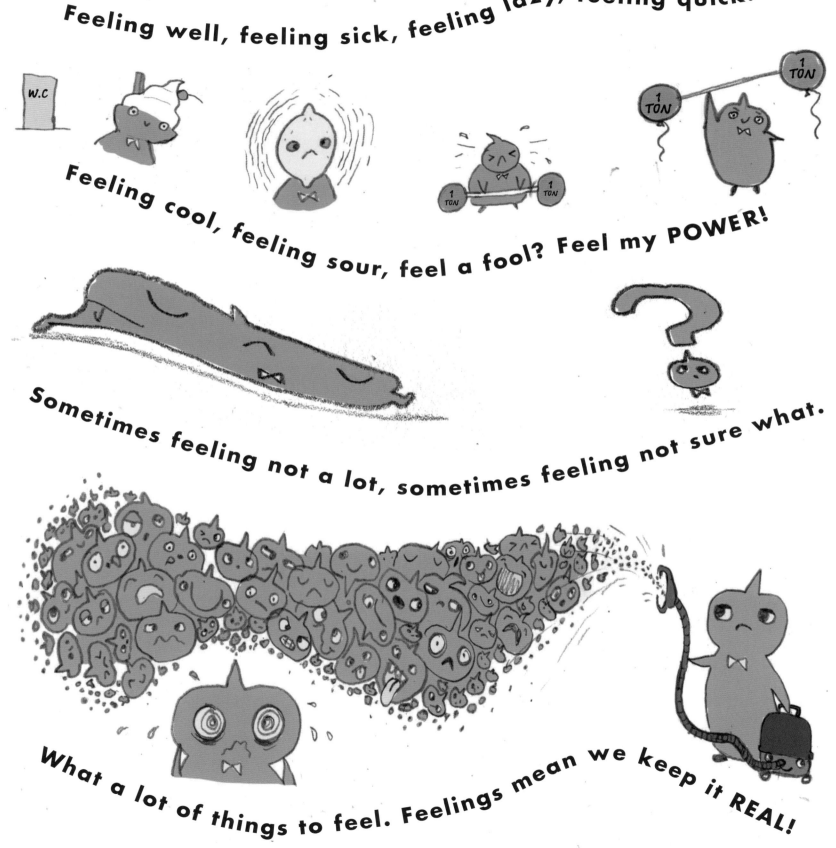

Feeling cool, feeling sour, feel a fool? Feel my POWER!

Sometimes feeling not a lot, sometimes feeling not sure what.

What a lot of things to feel. Feelings mean we keep it REAL!

# Body noises

Let's play the noisy game. Burp! We make all kinds of sounds when we are awake and even asleep!

heart beat

nails

WINNER!

NOISY GAME

START

clap

cough

whistle

Make any sound!

click

## How to play
A game for two or more players

1. Place your game pieces on **start**.
2. Take turns to throw the die and move around the board.
3. When you land on a sound, make that noise, then jump to the body part where it comes from (the matching color on the board).
4. When you land on a body part, go to the sound it makes.
5. When you land on "Make any sound!," make any body noise you like.
6. The first player to reach the end is the winner!

62

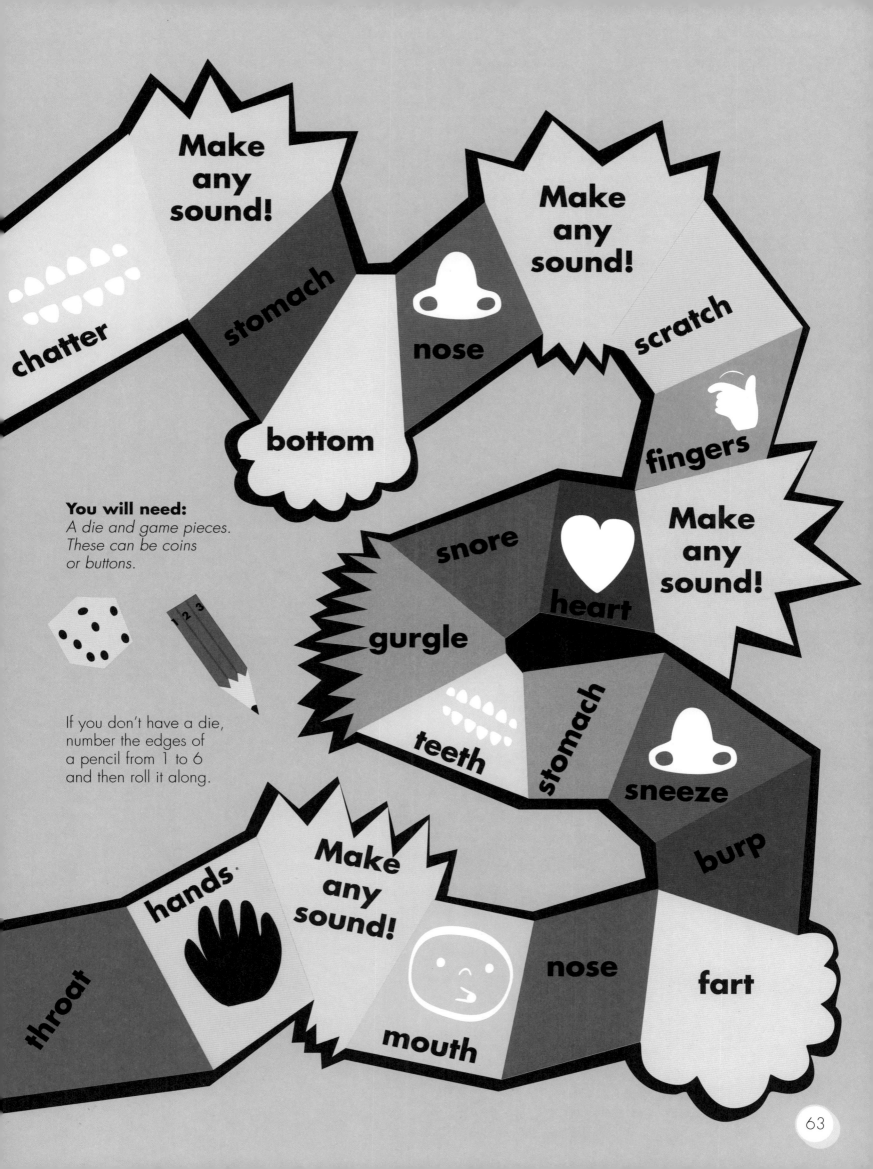

Make any sound!

chatter

stomach

nose

Make any sound!

scratch

bottom

fingers

**You will need:**
*A die and game pieces. These can be coins or buttons.*

snore

heart

Make any sound!

gurgle

stomach

teeth

sneeze

*If you don't have a die, number the edges of a pencil from 1 to 6 and then roll it along.*

burp

hands

Make any sound!

nose

fart

throat

mouth

63

# Index

Look up different parts of the body here and find out the pages they are on. Go through the alphabet to find the word you want.

First published in 2012 in hardcover in the United States of America by Thames & Hudson Inc., 500 Fifth Avenue, New York, New York 10110

thamesandhudsonusa.com

Library of Congress Catalog Card Number 2011938332

ISBN 978-0-500-65005-9

Published in Great Britain under the title My head-to-toe body book

Printed and bound in China by Imago

Produced by OKIDO
the arts and science magazine for kids
www.okido.co.uk

Written by Dr Sophie Dauvois
Illustration by OKIDO Studio: Alex Barrow, Maggie Li and Rachel Ortas
Design OKIDO Studio: Gigi Ho

Additional illustrations:
My brain, My hair, My teeth, Breathing, Going to the bathroom, Body hopscotch and Sleeping by Maggie Li
My senses, My heart and blood, How do I grow?, Staying healthy, Babies, My feelings, Body noises, Alex and Koko by Alex Barrow
My muscles and the explorers by Rachel Ortas
Spot the foods and Being sick by Mathilde Nivet
Busy body game by Soju Tanaka
My feelings and Staying healthy poems written by Gabby Dawnay

Special thanks to: Charlotte Brewin, Alice Tabuchi and Miqui Viars for their help; Edmund Fung for the Touch and Guess activity; Emil Gordon and Cleo Ferin for the Moustache postcard; and Emil Gordon and Sabrina Tabuchi for being astronauts.

Science consultant: Dr Jane Maloney, Institute of Education, University of London